Dedication

This book is dedicated to my wife Ester Doherty and my mother Lorraine Doherty

Acknowledgments

I would like to acknowledge and thank Prof. Paulette Laubsch for providing feedback and proofreading this book.

I would like to acknowledge Fairleigh Dickinson (FDU) Dean Kenneth T. Vehrkens who made so many opportunities possible for me in the fields of digital forensics, homeland security, emergency management, and computer security.

I would also like to acknowledge Dr. Kathy Stein-Smith and her staff at the Frank Giovatto Library on the Teaneck side of the Metropolitan Campus of FDU for their academic support to my students and me. We all appreciate the online journals and new features, such as chatting with a reference librarian.

Disclaimer

Dr. Doherty is an academic who is allowed to discuss various aspects of investigation and bring up anecdotes to help the reader learn various concepts, and discuss various aspects of computer forensic or mobile device investigation. A person reading this book should not conduct an investigation or direct others to unless they are both qualified and authorized to conduct such an investigation. It is also the responsibility of the reader of this book to learn about the regulations and laws in place for operating electronic equipment in their state or country or tribal land and what requirements are needed for private investigations. Investigations involving criminal matters or civil matters should be left to law enforcement professionals in that jurisdiction who are authorized to operate equipment and conduct investigations.

This book is an academic book discussing some anecdotes and thoughts about teaching digital forensic investigations of IPADS and desktop computers. It is not a complete discussion of the topic and is not a manual. It is only an academic discussion to teach principles to develop an interest in the subject but interested parties should then seek professional training and appropriate licensing procedures.

This book does not represent the opinions of Fairleigh Dickinson University or any school where Dr. Doherty previously worked. It is an academic work that examines computer forensics and IPAD forensics. This book was written to take an average reader and get him or her thinking about various aspects of investigation on desktop computers and IPADs and electronic communication over networks. The opinions expressed here do not officially represent any beliefs or opinions held by any committee, subcommittee, organization, employer, former coauthor, or former employer of the author.

This book will often display various types of digital forensic equipment and discuss some computer forensic services and methodologies. The author did not receive compensation for any picture or description of equipment. The book is not in any way, shape or form an official endorsement of those products or services but an example of equipment that was available at no additional cost to the author at the time of writing the book. The equipment or specific service discussed in this book does not mean it is the best of all related services or equipment. It was simply available at no additional cost to the author at the time of writing the book. It is also important to remember that one should never conduct any investigation without proper authorization from the official and lawful jurisdiction in the context of that situation.

Table of Contents

Chapter 0 – Identifying People and Computers

Computer Numbering Systems

You might ask me why I started the book with chapter zero. I did this to emphasize that one will often find that computer hardware or operating systems will start their numbering systems with zero unless they start with one [1]. It is also important for teachers and students to review the binary, decimal, and hexadecimal numbering systems. Humans use the decimal system. We count 0, 1, 2, 3, 4, 5, 6, 7, 8, 9, 10, 11, 12, 13, 14, 15, 16, 17, 18, 19, 20, and the pattern goes on. Everything that is transmitted or stored on the computer is made up of binary numbers. Bytes are the basic unit of measurement on computers and consist of groups of eight bits. A binary number is made up of bits consisting of 1s or 0s. It is a state of being on or off. The binary number 1111 is 15 in decimal. It consists of 1+2+4+8. The furthest bit on the right is 2 to the zero power. Professor Rex Barzee wrote a very nice book that may help teachers and students understand the binary numbering system and how to convert numbers from one system to another [2].

Fun Numeric Activity for People to do with Their Children

Hexadecimal systems use a base 15 numbering that go from 0 to F. Here is an example of hexadecimal counting: 0, 1, 2, 3, 4, 5, 6, 7, 8, 9, A, B, C, D, E, F, 10, 11, 12, and the pattern goes on. The binary number 1111 is F in hexadecimal and 15 in the decimal system. Parents and children may like creating a type of Rosetta Stone for themselves that show the numeric equivalents of binary, decimal, and hexadecimal numbers. The real "Rosetta Stone" can be seen in the British Museum in London, England, and shows one message in three different writing systems.

Humans Have Unique Identifiers (Biometrics)

The human has a fingerprint that can identify him or her to a computer. This is an example of what is called biometrics. "Galton published a book on the forensic science of fingerprints and claimed that the chance of two people having the same prints was about one in 64 million" [3]. That opinion suggests that the sole use of fingerprints may not be a 100% reliable means for computers to identify people as the world's population increases. A student once told me that he did not think facial recognition was a reliable means of identifying someone because facial transplants are possible. Here are some other thoughts on facial recognition / biometrics systems. Jason Mick wrote an interesting article for DailyTech and reported on some Vietnamese research about spoofing a facial recognition biometric system by using a picture of the person with the webcam [4]. That is why it is good to use more than one identifier, such as a password and a thumbprint. That is an example of multifactor authentication. Multifactor authentication is good for identifying the computer forensic examiner on his or her examination machine.

The Examination Machine
The Examination Machine is an isolated computer that is used for examining digital evidence. The examination machine should have a write blocker so that it does not change any evidence on an IPAD, cell phone, IPOD, disk, CD, or any other digital evidence that investigators may connect to the examination machine in an investigation. Digital Intelligence Corp. makes the FRED Station, which many people like as an examination machine. The examination machine may have a built in write blocker, and a cable connects from it to the IPAD. A program such as Lantern 4 by Katana Forensics may be run to pull all the information from the IPAD and examine it on the FRED Station. Once done, the examiner makes a report after reviewing the evidence.

MAC Addresses Are Unique Hexadecimal Identifiers Found on IPADS, Desktops, Etc.
People have unique identifiers on their body known as fingerprints. All desktops, IPADS, laptops, smart coffee makers, and anything else that connects to a network has a unique identifier called a MAC address. The MAC Address, also known as a Media Access Control address, is made up of 6 bytes of 48 bits. The MAC Address has 12 hexadecimal numbers.

Here is an example, 36:25:87: 44:A1:22. The examiner can use the website to lookup a MAC Address such as: www.macvendors.com and www.coffer.com, etc. A student once said that there exist tools to fake a MAC Address. This subject arises in computer security discussions. It may be a concern that requires further research.

Identifying Who is Calling You on the Phone – Spokeo, etc.
We often get phone calls by landline, cell phone, or a phone application on an IPAD. People have phone numbers registered to themselves. People may borrow a phone to call you or call you from a payphone. Spokeo can be used for the reverse lookup of phone numbers (see the URL www.spokeo.com). It is also a good idea to use more than one source to validate the account holder of a phone number. This is called "data validation."

Write blockers
Write blockers can be software programs that run and make the USB port act like a read only device. There are also hardware write blockers from companies such as Tableau. Here is a good link to look at https://www2.guidancesoftware.com/products/Pages/tableau/products/forensic-bridges/T6u.aspx that provides information on these products.

References

1. Doherty, et al. (2006), **"eForensics and Signal Intelligence for Everyone,"** Authorhouse Publishing, chapter 0.0, ISBN : 978-1-4259-6861-8(sc).

2. Barzee, R, (2014),"Really Understanding Binary," Published by Maia LLC, ASIN B00ODTQKM6

3. Knapton, S., (2014), "Why Your Fingerprints May Not Be Unique," The Daily Telegraph, April 21, 2014, U.K, URL Accessed 1/1/2016
   http://www.telegraph.co.uk/news/science/science-news/10775477/Why-your-fingerprints-may-not-be-unique.html

4. Mick, J., (2009),"Hackers Make Short Work of "Super-Secure" Facial Biometrics", Feb.18,2009, DailyTech
   www.DailyTech.com/Hackers+Make+Short+Work+of+SuperSecure+Facial+Biometrics/article14316.htm

Chapter 1 – Thoughts on Getting Started with Teaching IPADS Forensics

Introduction
This chapter is not a legal manual. This chapter is an academic discussion of a variety of digital forensic topics that a teacher or instructor may elect to teach in the classroom.

Exploring what is Meant by Digital Forensics
Digital forensics is basically the intersection of computer science and the law. It has to do the identification, preservation, analysis, and reporting of evidence to help support or reject a hypothesis or allegation of a crime.

Who is the Digital Forensic Examiner?
The digital forensic examiner, in my opinion, should be someone with training in computer science, investigation, the law, and the use of digital forensic tools. He or she should have the skills, education, experience, certifications, and training to do the job. The digital forensic examiner should be objective and look for exculpatory evidence to find a person innocent of the allegations as well as for evidence to support the allegations.

Why Should We Care About IPAD Forensics?
This is a good question posed by some young people. The answer is simple. IPADs may contain digital evidence that helps prove someone innocent or guilty in a court of law. Another reason is that IPADs are so prevalent in both American and Canadian society. Michael O'Grady tells us that 60 percent of residents of North America will have an IPAD by 2016 [1]. This large number of IPAD users is a very good reason to care about IPAD Forensics.

What is an IPAD?

A young student raised his hand and said that an IPAD is a tablet computing device that is made by Apple Computer. That sounds like a good working definition of an IPAD. We might want to go to the Apple website to get a more exact definition if we were writing a report that might be used in court. We may want to ask the assistance of a reference librarian. We should also be careful to identify what is not an IPAD. There are many devices that look like an IPAD but are not an Apple IPAD. You might run across an IPED or an Inkia InPad [2]. They may have a completely different operating system that is FAT 32 based and not an iOS operating system. This phenomenon occurs with many consumer electronic devices. One may go to New York City, for example, and find a street vendor selling Rollex watches that look like a Rolex watch but are only one percent of the true price. Some people refer to this phenomenon as "knock offs." We have to be aware of the types of knock offs that exist because they will use a variety of operating systems. That means that we must have a range of forensic tools to examine them.

An Example of a Subset of Possible Activities Done on an IPAD

It is important to know what kind of activities can be done with an IPAD before we think about examining one. IPADs are tools that can help people do great things. People can use an IPAD with Google Maps to plan a route to see grandma. An IPAD with an active wireless connection and an Internet browser can be used to look up products at the grocery store in order to make healthy choices. Children and adults can play electronic versions of board games, such as checkers and chess, so that time in the doctor's waiting room passes quickly. An IPAD could be used for displaying a shopping list while at the grocery store. It could also be used to videoconference with loved ones who live far away. The list goes on.

It is also important to understand that people can misuse an IPAD to do things that are against the law. Therefore, we need to consider some of these activities as well as the type of evidence that could exist there. People can use the camera to take a picture. Perhaps someone could take an unauthorized picture of a proprietary secret with one while visiting a research lab at a university and share it with a competitor. The camera in the IPAD can also be used for video conferencing. That means that inappropriate video and conversation with an adult and child is possible. That means a sex crime could take place with such a device. This emphasizes the need for parents to discuss Internet safety with their children.

People could surf the web and search for a wide range of things. Searches might be presented to help indicate intent to commit a crime. Perhaps someone was looking for ways to beat someone without leaving a mark. One could also use an IPAD for online gaming. Perhaps someone got into serious gambling debts by visiting an online casino and playing irresponsibly.

Someone could use an Excel spreadsheet on their IPAD to keep track of their illegal cigarette running business. There are often rumors of carloads of untaxed cigarettes purchased by senior citizens at Indian reservations and being sold for cash to avoid necessary fees, better known as taxes, that help fund sectors of the American government. An investigator may have to investigate such matters.

Locard's Principle of Exchange
Locard's principle of exchange says that when two objects come in contact with each other, both have changed. If Bill takes his IPAD to grandpa's house where an open wireless network exists, the IPAD will try to connect to grandpa's network. There will be evidence of Bill's visit on grandpa's wireless router log and on Bill's IPAD. If Bill connects his IPAD to his Windows 8 desktop computer, the registry will change on the Windows 8 computer. The IPAD may have changed since Bill probably dropped and dragged some documents and pictures from the desktop computer onto his IPAD.

A Brief Discussion of the IPAD 1

If you are going to be an IPAD expert, then you should learn about the history of the IPAD and know something about each generation of IPAD that is released for sale to the public. We techno-geeks probably all remember the release date of the IPAD 1 on April 3, 2010. You may consider such a device to be historic, but please remember that many people still use them. You can still find IPAD 1 devices for sale on eBay in 2016. That means that you need to know the specific software forensic tools can be used to investigate them.

It would also be advisable to know something about the hardware. The IPAD 1 had WiFi and an A4 processor with a clock speed of 1 gigahertz. It had a USB port and an iOS 4 operating system. Many of the files on an IPAD 1 had extensions such as M4V, MOV, MP3, MP3 VBR, MP4, and MPEG-4. That means that people may connect their laptop or desktop with an IPAD and share multimedia files such as movies or pictures. That also means that a digital forensic examiner should look for files on the IPAD and all the devices that connect to it. Since an IPAD has wireless capability, some evidence may be in a storage place such as a wireless hard drive hidden in the attic or in the iCloud.

It is important to think how this device is used and all the places where the digital evidence could be. Does the person have a webmail account on the IPAD? Is there a cloud storage site for the data? The list goes on. It is important to understand something about the level of computer sophistication that the IPAD user has, what devices he or she uses with the IPAD, and what activities are done on the IPAD.

A Brief Discussion of the IPAD 2

All of us techno-geeks could not wait for the IPAD 2 to reach the market. This device arrived on March 11, 2011, in 16, 32, and 64 Gigabyte versions. It is also important to remember that the unit of measurement for computers is bytes. Eight bits make a byte. A bit is unit of information that is either a 1 or 0, which more simply put as it is on or off. It is a charge or no charge.

The IPAD 2 had a newer iOS 4.3 operating system. It was also faster because it had the A5 processor. The resolution was 1024 x 768 pixels. This resulted in video games that were more realistic because the A5 processor could update everything more quickly. This also meant that the IPAD 2 was desirable to steal since it was desirable to use.

A Brief Discussion of the IPAD 3

This IPAD was really a breakthrough for the mobile computing enthusiast. It was released for sale on March 16, 2012. Do you remember hearing about the crowds sitting in lawn chairs outside the Apple store from the night before? The news reported about three million IPAD 3 devices being sold during the first week of its release. This model of the IPAD included a camera in the front of the unit as well as one in the back of the unit. The rear camera was five megapixels while the front was .3 megapixels. You might ask why the front camera was approximately 1/16 as powerful as the camera in the back. The front camera was designed to be used for video conferencing while the back camera was occasionally used for taking pictures at a graduation or of a trip to places like a national park. The more powerful rear camera could be used as a camcorder.

The IPAD 3 also had a retina display. This was a remarkable screen that allowed two people to put their IPADs side by side and play a game half on one screen and half on another. The other point that one should consider about the IPAD 3 is that it had a more advanced iOS operating system. It had a 5.1 iOS version of an operating system that could be later updated to version 7.11.

Unflod Baby Panda Virus Hits the IPAD 3

People undermined their IPAD 3 security by jailbreaking the IPAD 3 and installing applications that were not approved by the Apple store. When a person jailbreaks a computer or phone, they are trying to expand the usage of the device to levels not approved by the manufacturer. It is not surprising at all when a person gets a virus after undermining the security of the device and installing unknown applications. Absinthe 2.0 and Redsn0w were two programs that were available to jailbreak the IPADs. Unflod Baby Panda, also known as

Unfold Baby Panda, is malware that collects Apple IDs and passwords on some jailbroken iOS devices [3]. Gautam Prabahu wrote a nice article on this important subject, and individuals who would like more information on this can read his article [3].

A Brief Discussion of the IPAD 4
The IPAD 4 was released on November 2, 2012. This device had a 1 gigahertz A6 processor and a more powerful front camera that was increased to 1.2 megapixels. This could be used for higher quality videoconferencing. Many people used to bring their IPAD 4 to Fairleigh Dickinson University with their parents at graduation time to take pictures of the school and the flowers. It was my opinion that some people used the IPAD as a camera so that they did not have to bring another electronic device that had to go through the security scanner at the airport.

A Brief Discussion of the IPAD 5
The IPAD 5 was released on November 1, 2013. Students would bring their devices to the university and tell me that this device was revolutionary because it could act as a wireless hotspot for their other devices and for their friends. This connecting of other devices to a hotspot is known as tethering. The IPAD 5 had Bluetooth technology, and students often shared their friend's contacts between IPhones and IPADs. The digital forensic scientist in me could not help but think that some people might do risky activities that they would not normally do while tethered to someone else's connection. The IPAD 1-5 had a 9.7 inch screen, and it could be cumbersome for some people who liked small items that could be kept in coat pockets.

A Very Brief Discussion of the IPAD Mini 1
Some people liked a smaller device and the IPAD Mini 1 was that device. It had a 7.9 inch screen instead of a 9.7 inch screen. It could fit in some suit jacket side pockets and was more portable. The smaller screen appeared adequate for people doing messaging and social media applications.

A Very Brief Discussion of the IPAD Mini 2

This device was a significant improvement over the IPAD Mini 1. This device had a retina display with a screen that had a resolution of 2048 X 1536, which was better than the IPAD 1 and 2. This unit also had a dual core ARM Cortex A9 processor, which could help update the screen very quickly. It was popular with students.

A Brief Discussion of Understanding Hardware and Connectivity

It is important for people who will become digital forensic experts to be familiar with the various mobile devices that exist and what types of hardware they use. A retina screen and an A4 processor are examples of hardware. It is important to know the difference between an IPAD and an IPED.

It is also important to know what type of connectivity these devices have so that one knows to what these devices are connected. Can these devices connect to other devices as a hotspot with or without the owner's knowledge or permission? This familiarity will help the investigator understand how these devices are used or misused by others who capitalize on a careless user's mobile device.

A Very Brief Discussion of the Operating Systems

People often use words without knowing what they really mean. Operating system is one of those words. An operating system is basically a program that allows the user to manipulate the hardware and file systems of a computing device to do some type of activity. If one examines a variety of cell phones and IPADs, one will hear a variety of names of operating systems such as iOS, android, and many others too numerous to mention. It is best to read up on the various devices that are on the market and see what operating systems they use. Once that is done, you will be able to find some digital forensic tools that can be used to examine those devices and operating systems.

The IPAD uses the iOS operating system. The "iOS 7 User Guide – From A to Z – Tips, Tricks and all the Hidden Features for iPhone, iPad and iPod Touch" by Ryan Arturo might be a good book to start learning about what the iOS operating system capabilities are. It is important to learn about where to look for activities done on a digital device to help build a timeline.

A Discussion of Building a 24 Hour Timeline around a Crime that Involves an IPAD

Let us suppose that a person said that his IPAD was hacked, and as a result, $400.00 was taken from his bank account without his authorization. If we were investigators, we would want to know all the places where information about that account existed. Perhaps there was a paper copy of the bank account at home, and a post it note on the refrigerator had the password for the account. Perhaps there was a low security magnetic stripe ATM card with a weak password that was in his wallet and could have been read by a reader at a distance of up to 10 feet away. It would be good to talk to the victim and ask about who was in his house or apartment over the 24 hour period of time before the theft. The IPAD may not have been hacked at all, but the money being taken from the account could have been due to other bad security practices that were carried out by the victim that made this a crime of opportunity for someone.

If it seems that none of those other scenarios provides a possible lead, then the victim would probably talk one more time with the detective at his local police department and go over the report that was filed. The policeman might take the IPAD and have someone in the county prosecutor's computer crime unit to use a tool such as Lantern 4 or Oxygen Forensics for IPhones to examine the IPAD. It could be that the IPAD was jailbroken, for instance, and applications not authorized by Apple were on the IPAD and were shown to contain malware. The investigation might end if the malware and logs show connectivity with a remote country with weak or non-existent cybercrime laws. The amount of money stolen, the jurisdictions involved, the complexity of the crime, and the workload of the law enforcement agencies help decision makers decide what will happen next with the investigation.

IPAD Policies for Employees or Teachers

If a person was issued an IPAD for work, he or she probably signed a document that indicated that the device is owned by the school or corporation and that there is no expectation of privacy by the user. A policy should also be signed, dated, witnessed, and filed with human resources. This is important because it means that the organization can ask the user to surrender the device and examine it at any time. That also means that the organization may not need to involve the police and obtain a search warrant for looking at a company / school owned device that was issued to an employee who signed a policy that indicated that there was no expectation of privacy. There may exist some exceptions, so it is important to check first with the general counsel, authorized requestor, and human resources before seizing any equipment.

References

1. URL Accessed 10/22/2013 O'Grady, M., "Global Business And Consumer Tablet Forecast Update, 2013 To 2017" http://blogs.forrester.com/jp_gownder/13-08-02-global_business_and_consumer_tablet_forecast_update_2013_to_2017_0

2. Burns, M., "The Top Seven IPAD Knockoffs" URL Accessed12/25/2015 http://techcrunch.com/2010/05/28/the-top-seven-ipad-knockoffs/

3. Prabhu, G. (2014), "Warning Malware discovered on Jailbroken iOS devices which steals Apple ID and passwords" URL Accessed 12/26/2015 http://www.iphonehacks.com/2014/04/ios-malware-discovered-jailbroken-devices.html

Chapter 2 – Thoughts about Inspiring Middle School Children to be Future Digital Forensic Experts

The Value of Report Writing and Language Arts

Almost every year, I do presentations on robotics, computer forensics, or cell phone forensics for some middle school in New Jersey. I always ask the students what their favorite classes are and what classes they do not like. Many students tell me that they do not like language arts or English. Some say that they do not like history. I tell them that as someone in the computer forensics or robotics field, these classes are important. The students are surprised. I proceed to explain that we need to be able to write reports about how the robotics arm performed in a quality assurance test. We also need to write an instruction manual so others can use the robotic arm, too. It is important for computer scientists to be able to explain their products to marketing people and sales people as well. The need for report writing and expressing performance benchmarks is very important. Classes such as history and language arts may often help us develop the skills that we need to express ourselves on paper or verbally to a group.

The Value of Making Presentations in Language Arts Class

The students at one middle school had a data projector and a computer in front of the class where I did my presentation on computer forensics, cell phone forensics, and robotics. The students said that they had to do a PowerPoint presentation on a topic that they read about. I said that was great. I told the students that as a computer scientist and conference presenter, I often have to do PowerPoint presentations on various topics, such as the topic shown in figure 2.1. This is a skill that becomes very important. It is important to be able to know your audience and give a good presentation. The courses offered in middle school gives students an opportunity to hone this skill.

Figure 2.1 – Dr. Doherty Giving a Presentation of Teaching IPAD Forensics with a MOOC

I told the students about a time that I had to give a talk on the value of education in the workplace and options for completing one's degree. I said that the fact that I had to do oral book reports in grade school helped me with giving presentations. It is important to practice giving presentations and keeping to a time limit. It is also important to learn how to take questions and give answers. There is also a need to practice in dealing with hecklers and negative comments from the audience. I told them about a time that a friend gave a talk on dog bark analyzers for use with guard dogs. This fellow had very good slides that explained how a dog bark was recorded and analyzed by software to see if it was a friendly bark or if a hostile intruder was sensed. The dog walks around the facility and knows who should be there and who should not be there. Everyone listened carefully and watched the slides. Then there was a period for question and answers. One person said, "Ruff, Ruff, what kind of bark is that?" Everyone laughed, and the presenter did not seem adequately prepared for that type of question.

I told the students that I have made presentations at the WorldComp conferences, The High Tech Crimes Investigative Association (HTCIA) Conference, and various conferences that are part of the Association of Computing Machinery (ACM) organization [1,2,3,5,6,7,8,9]. It is important to remember that some people will agree with what you say while others will not. It is important to be able to gracefully take questions and criticism. It is also important to remember that some people may be jealous and give you a hard time because they wish they were giving a talk on a topic to others. When people speak to you, please consider the source.

Including Your Family on Trips
I was telling the students that it is important to spend time with your parents, brothers and sisters, and grandparents. I had a student of mine who did computer forensics for a living. This man was away from home for long periods of time where he was working in his office or away on investigations, using digital forensic tool training, or attending conferences in other states. He said that his wife and children were angry at him. His dog always liked him, but after many trips away, even his dog came over and bit him. I advised him to think about whether it was possible to go to a conference and bring his family, since it is good to spend your own money and give them a vacation while also being able to spend time with them.

Many computer scientists and some digital forensic experts attend and give talks at the Worldcomp computer conference. They bring their families with them. I gave a talk on teaching IPAD Forensics with a MOOC in figure 2.1 at the Monte Carlo Hotel in Las Vegas. I was able to bring my wife on frequent flyer miles, and we went at our own expense to see Red Rock Canyon and Hoover Dam after the conference. Another year, I went to conference, and after it was over, we stayed at our own expense again and went on a day trip to California. My wife took a picture of me in figure 2.2. on Santa Monica beach where "Baywatch" was filmed.

Figure 2.2 – Dr. Doherty on the Beach Where the TV Show "Baywatch" Was Once Filmed

The computer practitioners, investigators, students, and faculty that attend Worldcomp in Las Vegas represent people from 80 different countries. Many bring their families as a way of giving them a vacation and reducing the isolation that can occur from a profession that requires a lot of travel. At times, family members may even have an opportunity to meet people from other countries, which helps broaden their view of the industry that is so important to their spouse.

Co-presenting
I explained to the middle school students that the group presentations that they do in language arts class are also important. I once co-presented on the topic of malware with a former adult learner student named Don. Don also liked to share his important work with students [10]. It is important to learn how to co-present a topic with someone and give them an opportunity to speak. Some academics may act egotistical at times and try to usurp the student's good work. It is important to share the limelight and let others talk.

Speaking in Court
Since one role of the forensic investigator is giving testimony in court, I related to the middle school students the need to be able to express themselves in a stressful environment. In a court situation, it is necessary to describe the facts that you found in the exploration. That requires describing the facts as well as being able to accurately respond to any cross examination.

The Test Plan (An Abbreviated Sample of How One Investigates an Electronic Device)
Report writing is an important skill because digital forensic investigators may have to create a test plan for each device that they investigate. The test plan is a comprehensive document that shows how they will investigate the cell phone or IPAD. The test plan should have a section that has pictures of the device, documentation of the operating system type, and a model number / serial number. The test plan should also discuss what tools were used to examine the device and why those tools were chosen. The test plan should also have pictures or memory dumps of what was found and how that data were interpreted. Lastly, the plan should report what the outcome of the investigation was. (Additional information about test plans can be found in "Teaching IPAD Forensics" [11].)

If a person has a hard drive that is loaded with the forensic image of the phone or IPAD, then he or she should be able to use the tools and test plans to get the same results as the investigator. Some students will relate that they can see that their science class is also important because they have to follow procedures that are similar to the digital forensic investigator. There is often a "Eureka Moment" that occurs when students will see that Language Arts, English, Science, and history have value for the real world.

Conclusion
Students seem to value their class subjects more when they see a link between what they are learning now, how it relates to a job, and what its usage is in a high paying career.

Reference

1. September 21, 2010, High Tech Crime Investigative Association (HTCIA) Conference, in Atlanta, Georgia, gave a lecture in Marietta Hall of the Hyatt on, "Cell Phone Forensics for Law Enforcement and Private Industry

2. Doherty, E., (2013)," New Challenges in Teaching e-Forensics Online", 2013 International Conference on e-Learning, e-Business, Enterprise Information Systems, and e-Government (EEE'11: July 22-26, 2013, Las Vegas, Nevada, USA) has been accepted as a Regular Research Paper (RRP) - ie, accepted for both, publication in the proceedings on pages 67-71 and for oral formal presentation.

3. Doherty, E., (2012)," Teaching Mobile/GPS Device Forensics by E-Learning", 2012 International Conference on e-Learning, e-Business, Enterprise Information Systems, and e-Government (EEE'11: July 16-19, 2012, Las Vegas, Nevada, USA) has been accepted as a Regular Research Paper (RRP) - ie, accepted for both, publication in the proceedings and oral formal presentation.

4. Doherty, E., (2011),"Teaching Cell Phone Forensics and E-Learning", 2011 International Conference on e-Learning, e-Business, Enterprise Information Systems, and e-Government (EEE'11: July 18-21, 2011, Las Vegas, Nevada, USA) has been accepted as a Regular Research Paper (RRP) - ie, accepted for both, publication in the proceedings and oral formal presentation.

5. Doherty, E., (2011),"Teaching Digital Camera Forensics in a Virtual Reality Classroom," The 2011 International Conference on Computer Graphics and Virtual Reality (CGVR'11: July 18-21, 2011, Las Vegas, Nevada, USA) has been accepted as a Regular Research Paper (RRP) - ie, accepted for both, publication in the proceedings and oral formal presentation.

6. Doherty, E.P., Doherty, E.G., (2011), "E-Learning, Teaching Cell Phones Usage for Emergency Managers and First Responders, Conference: 2011 International Conference on e-Learning, e-Business, Enterprise Information Systems, and e-Government, (July 18-21, 2011, Las Vegas, USA)

7. Doherty, E. Cockton, G., Bloor, C., Benigno, D.,(2001)Improving the Performance of the Cyberlink Mental Interface with the "Yes / No Program", CHI 2001 Proceedings, Seattle, Washington, USA

8. Doherty, E., Cockton, G., Bloor, C., Benigno D., "Mixing Oil and Water: Transcending Method Boundaries in Assistive Technology for Traumatic Brain Injury, ACM Conference on Universal Usability, Washington D.C. USA, Nov. 16-17,2000

9. Doherty, E., Bloor, C., Cockton, G., Engel, W., Benigno, D., "Yes/No - A Mind Operated device for Severely Motor Impaired Persons" (2000), Computers Helping People with Special Needs, ICCHP 2000, Proceedings of the 7th International Conference on computers Helping People with Special Needs, July 17-21,2000 Karlsruhe, Germany

10. (2007), Computer Virus Detected, Recognition Camera Demonstrated *Inside FDU*, Retrieved From: http://inside.fdu.edu/otw/0711/happenings.html

11. Doherty, E., "Teaching IPAD Forensics Online with a MOOC,"2014 International Conference on e-Learning, e-Business, Enterprise Information Systems, and e-Government (July 21-24, 2014, Las Vegas, USA). Conference Proceedings, Pages35-39, ISBN 1-60132-268-2 - See more at: http://view2.fdu.edu/campuses-and-centers/center-for-cybersecurity-and-information-assurance/publications/#sthash.I1R2ZKA6.dpuf

Chapter 3 – An Example of Teaching Teenagers about Digital Evidence and Metadata

The Value of Classic Underlying Principles Such as Locard's Principle of Exchange

In my opinion, it is crucial for trainers or educators in the field of computer forensics to include material that cuts across the curriculum when teaching topics such as small scale digital device forensics. The reason is that students may one day be employed as investigators and will probably need to appear in court at some time in their career. Anyone who appears as an investigator or expert witness will tell you how difficult cross examination can be and how important it is to be prepared to discuss your field of expertise. That means the educator should start with basic forensic topics, such as Locard's Principle of Exchange that state that when two objects come in contact with each other, both objects are changed.

The Value of Understanding the Evidence

The 21st century provides us with many digital devices that we use to communicate or store information. Let's look at some. We know that people connect their IPhone to their IPAD by Bluetooth or WiFi. We also know that people transfer files across the iCloud, IPADs, IPhones, and computers. People also email files to friends or use webmail. Evidence can be deleted on one device but exist in others. It is impossible to talk about IPAD forensics without considering other devices and storage media with which the IPAD comes in contact.

The Iphone and IPAD both use an iOS operating system. Right now, we will focus on a cell phone. The cell phone, for example, can be used for calls as well as short text messages, email, and multimedia messages that have video included in them. This means that potential evidence to a case could lie in many forms within the file. The pioneer of forensic lab evidence, Mr. Locard, also said it was important to understand the evidence found because it held clues for the investigator about the activities at the crime scene [1]. To paraphrase the lessons taught by a detective / professor that I know, "To be ignorant of the evidence is to be ignorant of the crime."

An Example of the Diversity and Complexity of the Evidence

I taught a seminar about cell phone forensics to a group of teenagers and their teachers at Camp Discovery on the Hackensack Campus of Fairleigh Dickinson University. We examined a camera cell phone with simulated evidence from the crime scene. The first student said that we should preserve the evidence and identify it. She said that she was concerned that the pictures that were taken with the cell phone camera could have been emailed or sent as MMS attachments. She also said that the pictures could have been uploaded to a website and not emailed. I also said that the pictures should be hashed with an MD5 hashing algorithm so that the integrity of them would not be in jeopardy.

It is common to run a hash on a picture and get a large number with a tool such as WinMD5, which is shown in figure 3.1. WinMD5 is known as freeware and can be found online. There are many other tools that perform an MD5 hash pictures, too. If a picture was edited, it would have a new MD5 hash if we reran the WinMD5 program.

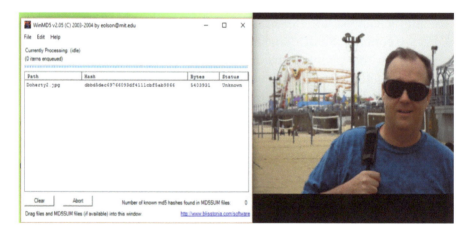

Figure 3.1 – Using MD5 to Perform a Hash Function on a Picture

A second student said that pictures could have been erased. That means we will need digital forensic tools that pass the FRYE Test, which is used in many states. The FRYE Test is a standard accepted by law enforcement, the legal community, and the academic community. This includes best practices and peer reviewed white papers. Some people feel that the Daubert Standard allows the judge to be the gatekeeper for forensic evidence in his or her courtroom.

Perhaps some of the photos were erased and written over. This means that we will have to use data carving tools such as File Extractor Pro, which is found in Data Lifter 2.0 or Adroit Photo Forensics. Data carving means that the software looks for the header and footer of a picture and tries to assemble the picture in a way that we may conceptualize it, which is similar to putting together a puzzle.

A third student said that some photos may exist on the phone that was not taken by the camera phone. I suggested looking at the metadata or the data that exists within the picture that tells about the camera focal length, resolution, type of camera used, and the date and time that the picture was taken. Metadata can be changed, but it probably exists in more than one place. A criminal would need to be very knowledgeable of computers or have access to an expert in order to change all metadata and related information concerning the picture. The chances are that altered metadata would show an inconsistency somewhere in the stored space on the computer.

Let's suppose I had a write blocker on my cell phone and collected the pictures to put on a hard drive. We never want to change evidence, so we would use a write blocker to prevent access times and other data to change on the phone that we were examining. If we look at figure 3.1 , we see that the metadata shows us that the picture was not taken with an IPAD. The picture in figure 3.2 was taken with a SONY digital camera that was a model DSC-W560. The exposure time was 1/1000 second, and the ISO speed was ISO-80. That EXIF metadata about the camera is revealed when I right click on the picture on a computer with a Windows operating system and select details. We could tell student 1 that this picture of Zabriskie's Point in Death Valley has metadata that indicates that this picture was probably taken with a Sony camera and not a cell phone. Why do I say probably? There could have been a genius that tampered with some metadata, so I don't like to say it is 100% absolutely from a Sony camera.

Figure 3.2 – Picture and Metadata

A fourth student was interested in the call logs. The phone has a log of who was called and of any calls received. The phone log also shows the duration of the call. Susteen's Secure View is a product that is very useful to obtain call logs and photos on a wide variety of cell phones. A guest lecturer who was a law enforcement officer also suggested going through the legal procedures to obtain a subpoena and give it to the telephone service provider for the cell phone. The reason is that it is good to obtain more information and do a comparison. Consider also that people may use a spoofing service that alters phone numbers. If time permits, it is great to ensure there are many checks and balances so that information found is of the highest quality.

A fifth student said that many young people SMS or short message service up to 144 characters to their friends. This student said that deleted or existing SMS messages may hold a key to activities at the crime scene. I suggested also using a second tool such as the Paraben Corporation's "Device Seizure" program in order to compare the results with Susteen's Secure View. Both products can sometimes recover SMS messages, and it is also possible that a lawyer will ask if we used more than one product to verify results. This provides a higher standard of validity to the information found.

If we say we only used one product, then it is possible that the lawyer may generate doubt about all evidence not being obtained. Perhaps other information may show that a person was not guilty. We know from serving as a jury member or watching television that even the smallest doubts can lead to an acquittal.

Other Places Digital Evidence Can Exist
It is also possible that digital evidence exists in many places at the crime scene. Let us now speculate on some of them. The victim or decedent may have a cell phone, beeper, thumb drive, PDA, SD Card, or even a hidden camera in a tie clip that stores frames a few times per minute, or transmits data elsewhere. The victim's small scale digital device may have also connected to a local area network or WiFi network. Perhaps routing tables on a local router show that the device in question communicated with someone else. Devices that are connected to a network often have unique identifiers as an IMEI, SN, or MAC Address. The MAC address is a unique identifier that is associated with a particular networked device such as a Personal Digital Assistant (PDA). Some PDAs can also be used to make phone calls.

Let us now discuss the serial number, SN. It may be found in multiple places on a PDA or vintage cell phone. The serial number may exist on a bar code found underneath the battery. This bar code may be read by a bar code reader such as the ones found at the supermarket or library. The serial number may also exist in another location on the device, such as on a sticker, as well as in the buffers associated with the device's operating system.

If someone was emailed, SMSed, or called, then digital evidence should exist on the destination cell phone, laptop, PDA, netbook, or desktop computer of the person who was called. The Internet Service Provider (ISP) and telephone service provider of the other party may also have to be subpoenaed in order to obtain all the relevant data.

Mapping Metadata and Checking the Accuracy of a Location
There is something known as EXIF metadata with the camera or camera phone. This becomes embedded in a digital picture. Some IPADs and camera phones have a geotagging feature that may be turned on, and this will embed GPS coordinates in pictures. An example of such a picture is Figure 3.3, which was taken at the Information Assurance Center at 1921 Las Lomas Road, NE at the University of New Mexico. Figure 3.4 shows the location of the GPS metadata on a map. Then we can compare the known location of the picture with the mapped metadata location.

Figure 3.3 – Taking a Picture at a Known Location & Establishing a Benchmark

It is also good to check the metadata of the picture and compare it to the specifications of the device from which it came. If the resolution of a picture was 640 x 480 and that device does not support that specific resolution, then that picture originated from another place other than that device. Compelson's Camera Ballistics is a good tool to check the probability of a picture being taken from a certain device. One should also look at the pictures carefully to see if there was any inconsistency that might suggest photo editing. If there is such an indication, then a closer look will be needed.

Figure 3.4 – The Mapped Location of the Metadata

The mapped location of the metadata for this test seems to be very close, if not exact, to the location where the picture was taken. We have to remember that this picture was taken in an open sunny area with a clear view of satellites in the sky. Results may differ in other locations due to access to satellites in the sky. Other issues that may impact the mapping might include cloud cover, tall buildings, or significant amounts of metal surrounding where the photo was taken. It is important to validate your tools and try to determine their accuracy.

Tailoring Your Talk to the Needs of Your Audience
The Camp Discovery group of which we just spoke was very interested in the legal aspects of search and seizure as well as the procedures to make evidence available to both sides in a trial. Determining what evidence will be used in the trial is known as the discovery process. The fact that the students asked about this could be attributed to the students watching so many television shows on cable television about lawyers such as Boston Legal, Law and Order, Perry Mason, and Matlock.

A few months prior to the Camp Discovery experience I did a similar seminar for another population of people who asked that my discussion of legal topics be minimized and that the focus for the presentation be more on the use of the cell phone forensic software packages as well as the minimum hardware requirements for the examination machine. The point is that you need to tailor your material to fit the requirements of those who are in your seminar or class.

References
1. Harrill, D., Mislan, R., (2007), "A Small Scale Digital Device Forensics ontology", Small Scale Digital Device Forensics Journal, Vol. 1, No. 1, June, 2007

Chapter 4 - Examples of Building a Digital Forensic Examiner Resume

The Motivation for Giving Examples of Each Resume Building Topic

It is easy to discuss things in very general terms to students or an audience. Students sometimes request specific examples of education, classes, or organizations that they can join to enhance their digital forensic resume. The goals and motivation for writing this chapter is to give specific examples of information that should be included in one's resume, such as certifications, classes, and organizations that students can seek to join in order to increase the strength of their digital forensic resume. The goal is not to advertise specific products or promote any entity over another. It is important to remember that there are a plethora of good organizations, certifications, and vendor training as well as webinars from which people can choose.

An Example of Discussing Digital Forensic Resume Building with Students

Sometimes, a graduate student in the Master of Administrative Science program at Fairleigh Dickinson University (FDU) will ask how he or she can build his or her resume in digital forensics. I tell them that there are many things that one can do while one is in school to try to build one's knowledge, education, skills, training, and experience in this field. It is also important to network with people in this field, too.

Examples of Digital Forensic Clubs or Special Interest Groups

Universities, colleges, technical schools, high schools, and some grade schools have after school clubs or special interest groups where people can learn about various topics or careers. These organizations are usually free and allow the student to get hands on training or learn things from someone knowledgeable in that field. An example of this is FDU's "Digital Forensics Special Interest Group (DFSIG)". It meets once a week for approximately seven to ten weeks each semester for about one hour. It is open to faculty, staff, and students.

One topic is learning to wipe a hard drive. Some students learn to use a Logic Cube to accomplish this before using the hard drive to capture simulated suspect evidence. Students always ask, "Why do I have to wipe a new drive that just arrived from the factory?" The answer is that there is a small possibility that it might have malware on it [4]. It is better to wipe the drive and eliminate any doubts about what was there before. We also learn to do some basic skills in IPAD forensics, computer forensics, or cell phone forensics. One of these basic skills is to put the device in a Faraday Bag in order to block all connectivity to the device from all outside devices.

The Value of Digital Forensic Classes with Practitioners
One time, I took a class on digital forensics with the Public Agency Training Council (PATC) in Las Vegas. I discussed the Faraday Bag and the DFSIG with a few of them. One investigator told me that putting the IPhone device in airplane mode and then in a Faraday Bag might be a better option because things in Faraday Bags may keep trying to connect to the outside world. When the device cannot reach anything, it will increase the power of the signal and thus deplete the battery and volatile evidence. He said it is good to make note of putting it in airplane mode and then in the Faraday Bag in the chain of custody form and explain why it was done. That was a great insight and a valuable conversation for an academic like me.

Some students and investigators who have some upcoming vacation time and G.I. Bill benefits have said that they will take some type of GPS, cell phone forensic, or IPAD forensic training from either the Berla Corporation, Paraben Corporation, the PATC, or Katana Forensics. Students see the value of networking with digital forensic practitioners and learning about real life tips in class. They also learn about digital forensics from people who sit in both the training world and the active investigation world. As they do this, they can also find out which states and agencies are growing and which ones are stagnant or downsizing. It is also good to collect business cards. A person who makes a good impression as an honest, hard-working, and intelligent student may learn about a future part time or full time opening somewhere.

A student who goes to a PATC class or Paraben class and satisfactorily completes all the in-class activities could get some type of certificate of attendance. Certificates of completion are important to collect as one advances in this field. An individual should put all of these types of certifications in a file so they are available when seeking a job. In addition, attending such training should be included on the person's resume.

An Example of Continuing Education
Continuing education is a low cost investment in terms of money and time, but it can yield some good results. Dr. Doherty teaches a three hour "Introduction to IPAD Forensics" continuing education class at FDU. In 2015, the cost of this class was $50. This covered the cost of educational materials and a demonstration of tools that could be used. A certificate of attendance was provided at the end of the course, Some students who already know a lot about IPAD forensics take a continuing education class in order to get a certificate and to log hours in relevant training in order to keep a certification current.

An Example of a Symposium
Since 2013, FDU has had a yearly Information Assurance Symposiums. Digital forensics and IPAD forensics are included as part of the agenda of the program. In addition, appropriate speakers who focus on related topics are part of the program. For example, in 2015, the theme of the symposium was Law Enforcement and Cyber Defense, and the keynote speaker was from the Central Intelligence Agency and spoke of Living in Cyber Space. Symposiums are a way to learn about new trends in the field of Information Assurance and informally network with people from intelligence agencies, corporations, and local law enforcement agencies. One can learn about new advances in best practices as well as possible leads for new job openings.

Keeping Track of Improvements to Your School's Accreditation or Awards

"Congratulations! Fairleigh Dickinson University has been re-designated as a National Center of Academic Excellence in Cyber Defense Education (CAE/CDE). Our "enhanced" cyber academic programs are duly recognized by NSA and DHS. Fairleigh Dickinson University's re-designation is valid till 2020" [3]. This type of academic designation may improve the perceived value of your education to a potential employer. It may also be good to mention if you are ever going through the process of "voir dire" and trying to qualify in court as an expert witness.

An Example of a Conference

The PFIC Conference sponsored by the Paraben Corporation is a good way to learn about new trends in digital forensics and best practices, and to get training on tools that could help in computer, IPAD, and cell phone investigations. It is also an informal opportunity to speak to people on the prosecution and defense sides of the house about their opinions.

The International Association of Computer Investigative Specialists (IACIS) is another organization that has conferences, gives training, and helps people in getting certified in certain areas of digital forensics.

The HTCIA, also known as the High Tech Investigative Association, is another great organization where one can go to conferences, meet vendors, see digital forensic equipment demonstrated, and learn about new topics in digital forensics.

An Example of a Webinar

There are many good webinars that are available free online or for a relatively low cost if one registers for the session. Guidance Software, the makers of Encase, provides webinars on a wide range of topics that interested individuals can sign up for.

The PATC has webinars that last from one to four hours and may cost from $99 to $299. One example that comes to mind was a webinar in which I was very interested. On October 23, 2015, there was a digital forensic Oxygen Forensics webinar that included a basic license for the software, some type of certificate, and good training [1]. Oxygen forensics works with many iOS operating system devices.

I would recommend checking with PATC and ask if that webinar will run again and what version of Oxygen software will be given with the class so that there are no misunderstandings about what investigation software is given to the student. The Oxygen Forensics website shows that there exists an Oxygen Forensics for IPhone that can be used with the following: iPhone, iPhone 3G, iPhone 3GS, iPhone 4, iPhone 4S, iPhone 5, iPhone 5c, iPhone 5s, iPhone 6, iPhone 6 Plus, iPad, iPad 2, New iPad 3, iPad 4, iPad Mini, and iPod Touch. This version of software may or may not be available with the webinar so it is imperative to check first before signing up for a class. In any case, webinars are great ways of learning for busy people who cannot fly out to a class and spend a few days away from the office.

Getting Real Experience in Digital Forensics
One way of getting experience in digital forensics is to work for a divorce lawyer or private investigator on a part time basis. In many states, lawyers who passed the bar for their state and are practicing law already have a private investigator's license. Some certified computer examiners told me that it was their opinion that it is best for you to start working for lawyers part time because you would be under their employment and under their protection if a lawsuit occurred about the investigation you helped perform. Many lawyers and private investigators are more willing to try out people part time because they do not have to pay a salary and benefits, and can easily terminate their employment if things do not work out.

An Example of an Organization of Interest to Educators and Students - NMIA

The National Military Intelligence Association is also a good organization for educators and students who are interested in intelligence. Intelligence can also include elements of cyber and digital forensics. They have a yearly conference that includes great speakers and vendors who have display tables set up. The networking opportunities at such a conference are amazing.

An Example of an Internship

There may be internships available with government agencies, corporations, or with lawyers. The Central Intelligence Agency (CIA) website is worth checking out. There are sometimes summer programs and scholarships available for people who are studying digital forensics. It would also behoove students to check the HTCIA, IACIS, and other organizational websites to see what internship or part time employment opportunities exist for students.

Certifications

It is also good to build one's resume with certifications. Certifications help demonstrate that a person has a specific common body of knowledge for a particular skill. If I was considering IPAD forensics certification, then Oxygen Forensics, Cellebrite, Katana Forensics and XRY Forensics would be good choices to contact about certification classes and tools with regard to IPhones and IPAD forensics. It is also important to remember that particular certifications become recognized in a way similar to "branding" in consumer markets. It would behoove the student of digital forensics to seek certifications from: XRY Forensics, Katana Forensics, Oxygen Forensics, and Cellebrite as well as from any other easily recognized vendor of digital forensic tools.

An Example of a Higher Education Program That Includes Digital Forensics

The Master of Administrative Science Degree at Fairleigh Dickinson University is a program that teaches students about a wide variety of leadership, management, and technical topics. It also has a group of digital forensics classes that can lead to a certificate. Let's examine some possible opinions why people are pursuing master's degree level programs. Perhaps some people have the opinion that the four year college degree is so commonplace that a master's degree is needed to help differentiate oneself from the group. Others may like learning and wish to study something in depth. There are many wonderful master's degree programs in the United States, and it would be impossible to discuss them all.

I will discuss FDU since it is a program with which I am most familiar. If one takes six classes in the computer security and forensics administration area and four additional classes, it is possible that one can graduate with both a certificate in computer security and forensics administration and a Master of Administrative Science degree. It is important to note that some of the people who take the computer security and forensic administration classes are presently unemployed people who are planning to apply for jobs in a government agency or a corporation after they graduate. Some of the students are also adult learners who have returned to school after finishing their undergraduate degrees in the late twentieth century.

To earn this certificate, students need to complete six of the following courses, or 18 credits.

Computer Security and Forensic Administration (18 credits)

> MADS 6637 – Computer Systems Seizure & Examination
>
> MADS 6638 – Computer Security Administration
>
> MADS 6639 – The Forensic Expert.
>
> MADS 6654 – Forensics Administration
>
> MADS 6697 – Current Issues in Cyber Forensics
>
> MADS 6701 – Special Topics: Intro. To Computer Network Security

41

MADS 6702 – Special Topics: Investigation of Comp.
System/Network Emergencies

MADS 6730 – Malware Investigations

MADS 6735 – Introduction to Countermeasures for Malware

MADS 6773 – Current Issues in Forensic Sciences

Two students who were unemployed told me that their opinion was that young employers value a recent college degree in something technical over something from a half century ago. It would behoove the person with an old four year technical degree to consider getting a master's degree and also including a certificate in computer security and forensics administration.

Publishing

One way to enhance your resume in digital forensics is to publish something. You can write a four or five page paper on a digital forensic topic and submit it for consideration to be published. The WorldComp Conference, which meets in Las Vegas, Nevada, is considered the largest academic computer conference in the world. They also have a subconference called "SAM," which has to do with topics related to computer security and management [2]. It is also important to remember that computer forensics and mobile device forensics, which includes IPADS, is a subset of security topics. There are many conferences that publish papers, and it is good to research such publications. The IEEE often has opportunities for publishing, and they are worth contacting for more information.

Writing books are more time consuming, but this is also another way to enhance one's resume. One can self-publish with a publisher such as AuthorHouse or Lulu or go with an academic books publisher such as CRC Press.

Volunteering

One can also volunteer for organizations, such as the HTCIA, or volunteer to help at a conference. This is a good way to get known and to be able to attend events at a low or no cost. Volunteering can also make oneself feel good about giving. It is good to give back to the community by doing something for free for the good of others. Such kindness is encouraged by many cultures and the person who gives his or her time not only feels happy about giving, but is respected by those who know of the volunteering.

Downloading Free Tools and Practicing

Many students will download free forensic tools such as Helix 3 and practice imaging a computer hard drive. Imaging a hard drive means copying all the allocated and unallocated free space on that drive so that one has an exact clone after the process is completed. People will also practice using Helix 3 to image the existing RAM on the computer. Practicing with real tools on old hardware at home is a good way to develop real life skills.

Conclusion

There are many ways to enhance one's resume in the field of digital forensics. There are webinars for the busy professional. There are conferences, symposiums, continuing education classes, and short intensive classes put on by groups, such as the PATC or Paraben, employers, and educational institutions. One may also join an organization such as the HTCIA, NMIA, ASIS International, the IACIS, and many others to get training and learn about job openings. One can get experience working part time for a lawyer or private investigator. It is also good to try out digital forensic tools with your own hardware and practice recovering things. Publishing is good too if you have something new to add to the common body of knowledge in digital forensics. You could take formal classes in a master's degree program too. There are many ways to improve a resume, but it all starts with getting out of your recliner chair and doing something.

References

1. URL Accessed 12/26/2015
    http://www.patc.com/online/1062.shtml

2. URL Accessed 12/26/2015 http://sam.udmercy.edu/sam15/

3. URL Accessed 1/3/2016 http://view2.fdu.edu/campuses-and-centers/center-for-cybersecurity-and-information-assurance/

4. Hughes, A., "Malware Found On New Hard Drive," (2007) URL Accessed 1/6/2016 http://www.zdnet.com/article/malware-found-on-new-hard-drives/

Chapter 5 – Anecdotes of Teaching Adult Learners about Digital Forensics

Background

Graduate classes at Fairleigh Dickinson University (FDU) can be taken in person or online in a virtual platform that is also known as a webcampus. Some classes are known as hybrid and include both the traditional "bricks and mortar" campus and a webcampus component. I am fortunate to teach both modes as well as in person continuing education.

Continuing education classes for cell phone forensics, IPAD forensics, and Legacy Device Forensics are also marketed to people around New Jersey. I have been teaching the continuing education class, "Introduction to IPAD Forensics," since 2013. At the graduate level, I have been teaching "Computer Seizure and Examination" and many other digital forensic and computer security classes since 2005. As we know, the IPAD was not invented until 2010. Please keep this in mind as you read this chapter so that you can understand my perspective.

A Look at Some Mature Learners that I Teach in Class

I often teach graduate classes such as "Current Issues in Cyber-forensics," "Computer Security Administration," "Malware Investigations," "Computer Seizure and Examination," "Introduction to Countermeasures for Malware," and "Introduction to Computer Network Security."

These classes will often include a mix of National Guard students, law enforcement students, and people who are returning to school after being recently unemployed from a successful career. Then there are the other student types that are less common, such as the "Returning Senior Citizen Learner."

The Recently Unemployed Student Who Had a Successful Career
Many students with long successful careers often find themselves out
of work as many companies undertake outsourcing as a way to reduce
costs and increase profits. In some cases, a company may be sold to
another company that cannot or does not choose to absorb all the
employees within the organization.

I first noticed recently unemployed people that had high paying
successful careers returning to school about the time of the "Financial
Crisis of 2007-2008." Here is one anecdote that stands out in my
memory. I remember a potential student coming to sit in a chair in
front of my desk in 2008. He was dressed in an expensive tailor made
suit. Let's call him "the suit." He said that he was working in a large
city and previously made a very large salary. He said that he was only
a decade from retirement, out of work, and that nobody would ever
give him that type of money again. He said that he felt that computer
forensics would be a new career that he would like to pursue. He said
that he knew that he would only start with only a fraction of what he
made before, but that was okay.

He said that he did a literature review before visiting me and told me
that it was his opinion that computer forensics or mobile device
forensics was a career path that was open to any aged person with the
right skills who could do the job. I agreed that this was the case with
some computer forensic investigation companies that have called me
on the phone and asked me if I have any "star students" who also have
some hands on skills and wish to start work part time in this field. The
technical people from these companies that are seeking talented
student workers also said that age is no barrier. This type of student
that I just described is often looking for continuing education so that
he or she can quickly get some of the hands on skills in some area of
digital forensics and to network with others in class to obtain
information about jobs and learn about present employment trends.

As mentioned before, continuing education is a low cost investment and a good way to explore digital forensics. If the student likes the continuing education, he or she will often be interested in a for credit class that has a digital forensics or investigation focus so that he or she can also learn some of the theory behind using the digital forensic tools.

The fellow that I mentioned before, "the suit," had completed many continuing education classes in digital forensics and a few classes at the graduate level. He kept networking with everyone that he could and later obtained a private industry job. This job seemed to be part information technology and partially incident response. He did not make the salary that he did, but it was a happy ending for him.

Another memorable anecdote was from seven years later and follows a similar pattern. This fellow, who we will randomly assign the fictional name "Bob," sat down at my desk. He was out of work after a successful high tech career. He said that he was highly paid and would not find that type of job again since most of that work was outsourced. He was a decade away from retirement and had lots of financial obligations. Bob took a few of the continuing education classes that I taught regarding digital forensics. He also completed a digital forensic or investigation class like the "suit." Bob did a literature review, too. Bob did one thing better than the suit. Bob went to many low cost or free training opportunities that were provided by academia. He networked furiously with other people and got a job after his first graduate school class was done. The new job did not pay as much money as what he made before. The job was not what he expected, but it was a great opportunity to go in a new direction and was a happy ending for him.

I often hear from so many people that we can expect to have at least three different careers in our lifetime. In some cases, the number of careers might be close to six or seven. Because of this, all of us must ensure we have the skills and knowledge needed for the next job, and not just for the job in which we currently are.

The Returning Senior Citizen Learner
This type of learner is my favorite type of student. This person is usually highly motived, has lots of time, and is very interested in learning. This type of person usually has a very rich background and adds a lot of value to any class with significant participation in class. This type of person also alleviates the fears of students who are often in their late forties or early fifties and returning to school after being away from school for 20 to 25 years. A senior citizen learner was in computers since the early days of mainframes in the 1960s and was still actively using laptops and mobile devices. He also saw a connectivity of old and new technology since some old organizations with old legacy computer equipment still use and integrate those items with new technology systems. We had a simulated crime scene with old and new equipment. We had a Dell Inspiron from 1998 with USB 1.0, a modern Dell Laptop, a switch, a wireless router with Ethernet ports in the back, and Ethernet cables. We also had a variety of old and new digital media, which included a 3.5 inch floppy disk, a CD, and a USB drive. All these items could be easily integrated together in class and simulate an environment of three generations in one home. We practiced wiping practice drives and then forensically imaging the desktop computer's hard drive with a Logic Cube. We practiced imaging the RAM and the Laptop hard drive with Helix 3.

Something Great about the Twenty-First Century
One thing that adult learner students often tell me is that they are glad that they live in the twenty-first century. We know that we are living longer. Our students recognize this and identify the impact on their careers. Most individuals who retire from their primary career are not ready for full-time retirement. These men and women say that they want to keep learning and have a new part time career after they retire from their present job. They tell me that they are not ready to spend every day sitting around a pool in Florida, or sitting in a rocking chair and looking at the world go by. This new part time career is something that they envision as fun. The fun career includes investigation, IPAD forensics, desktop computer forensics, or performing forensic images at remote sites.

Two men who are graduate students in my classes told me that they often show their grandchildren their grades from the university and that this creates new channels of communication. Of course, many students have grandchildren who are quite adept with computers and the different systems and show their grandparents how to do some of the things they need to know.

Computer Forensic Shows
There are a variety of computer forensic shows around the United States. One might attend the Computer Forensics Show / Cybit Expo in New York. I have attended the Computer Forensics Show in Washington, D.C., and felt it was great. I told the adult learners that computer forensic shows are a great way to talk to vendors who make a variety of computer forensic tools and to see those tools demonstrated. Any attendee can pick up specification sheets about digital forensic tools, ask questions about training / certification, and ask vendors informal questions that would not be possible during a regular sales call. Computer forensic shows usually have good speakers and provide forums where people can ask questions.

Chapter 6 – Imaging an IPAD in Class

Introduction

This chapter simulates some interaction that may happen in class when a student plays the role of a corporate IPAD examiner and some of his / her classmates want to play other roles to help acquire, analyze, and report on the digital evidence in an IPAD. The names are fictional and randomly assigned to characters in this simulated exercise. In order to keep the book size small, only some print screens of the entire IPAD simulated evidence seizure process are shown.

Wilma is the Authorized Requestor (AR) who starts the corporate investigation.

Bob, Maria, and Pat are students who assist on the incident response team.

Mr. D. and Ms. L. are adult learners / senior citizen students who play the roles of inspectors and compliance / regulatory experts in a corporation.

Wilma asks, "Bob, did you call HR and make sure there are signed policies for the IPAD and computer usage?"

Bob says, "Yes, HR has signed and dated copies of the policies that the employee read, and we have a print screen of a banner on the IPAD stating that it was the property of the company and that there was no expectation of privacy."

Maria says, "I have filled out a chain of custody that has my name, the date, time, case number, and reasons that this IPAD is being seized, and I made sure the other fields on the form were filled out correctly according to the instructions of the general counsel."

Bob says, "I asked the employee to surrender the IPAD and step away from the simulated crime scene."

Pat says, "I have a cell phone. I also have a research machine that is connected to the Internet, and I can download manuals, forms, and seek information on anything that we have questions about."

Bob says, "I have a test plan that has print screens, also known as screen shots, of the licensing information about our tool. The test plan also describes how we will validate our investigation tool and why we chose it. Our test plan discusses the strategy of investigating an IPAD and how we will interpret the evidence."

Maria said, "I have my examination machine here, and it is not connected to the Internet. I turned off my Bluetooth, Wifi, Infrared, and disconnected my Ethernet cable and modem cable. "I also put in a CD and ran the anti-virus and anti-spyware software. We are disconnected from the outside world and free of malware that could taint our evidence."

Pat said, "I will turn on the airplane mode and connect the IPAD in the Faraday Bag with a cable to the examination machine. I am ready to speak to HR and the general counsel about the possibility of obtaining a compel order from the local judge in case the suspect does not want to give us the password for the IPAD."

Bob starts Oxygen Forensics on the examination machine, and one can see the progression.

Figure 6.1 – A Registered Copy of Oxygen Forensic Suite

Figure 6.2 – The Oxygen Forensic Extractor

The Oxygen Forensic Extractor pictured in figure 6.2 is nice because one can use an auto device connection mode or one can manually select the device. It is really a personal preference which one to choose, but I think some people may like the auto mode if he or she thinks that the information about the device that they have is incomplete. Other people like to be in control of every piece of information and type everything in by himself or herself. It is also important to remember to think, slow down, and do all the steps carefully. Any type of investigation of digital evidence could go to court, and it is important to remember that small mistakes could hurt a case and the reputation of the examiner.

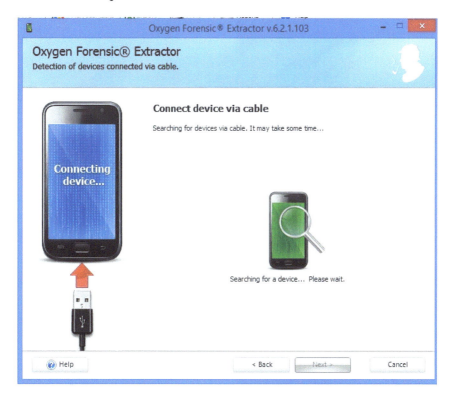

Figure 6.3 – Indicator to Connect a Cable

The indicator to connect a cable is a good thing. It lets you know that this is the step where a cable is connected from the IPAD or IPhone to the examination machine. It is good that there are updates and graphics to assure the investigator of what is going on. I personally like the magnifier that circles around the device because I know that work is being performed, and the process has not stalled. It is my opinion that the screens simplify the process of digital evidence seizure and also give the students more confidence that they can do this.

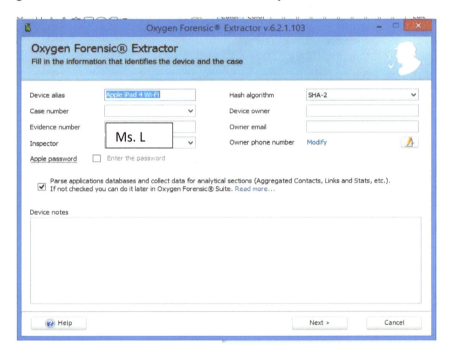

Figure 6.4 – The Report Wizard

This report wizard pictured in figure 6.4 is very helpful because it prompts the investigator or the student learner to input all the data so that it becomes easier to create a neat report. Contact information and passwords can also be entered so that they are stored for future usage and do not get misplaced.

Mr. D gives the students some good relevant perspective from his many years around computers and says, "This input of passwords and other data is important because years ago in the early days of mobile device forensics, investigators had to manually investigate devices without automated software tools. Passwords written on small slips of paper, in my opinion, could possibly be separated from devices that were logged in as evidence. A trial might be years later."

The print screen in figure 6.4 shows us that there is also a section for notes, which is really important. One may have something important to say now as one is making the report, but the trial may not come up for years. The notes are an important memory aid. The hash algorithm in the picture says SHA-2. It is important to remember that MD5 is not the only existing hash and that other hash algorithms are possible.

Figure 6.5 – Seized Data (Redacted for Book)

The Figure 6.5 shows that Oxygen Forensics has obtained the model, which is the Apple iPad 4 WiFi and the IMEI. The IMEI was redacted, and we must always remember that there are a variety of privacy laws. This IPAD is school property and did not seem appropriate to share that information for the book. The Apple Boot Loader information is also shown.

Figure 6.6 – The Data Selection Screen

This "Data Selection Screen" depicted in figure 6.6 is an extremely important screen because it allows the student or investigator the opportunity to select what data or evidence needs to be extracted from the IPAD. The options include the event log, calendar, file structure, images, audio, video, documents, applications, database files, and other files. Files from internal memory can also be chosen. It is important to remember that in a special case, a judge might order the investigator to only look at the pictures. Having options to only collect certain evidence is very important.

This screen also simplifies the evidence collection process, in my opinion, and helps students gain confidence that they can do this.

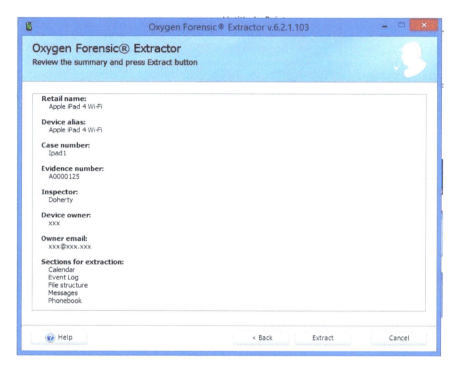

Figure 6.7 – The Brief Summary Before Extraction Screen

This "Brief Summary Before Extraction Screen" is one of my favorite screens because it summarizes what I am collecting before I collect it. This screen tells me about the basic information about the device and gives me one more chance to think about it before I collect the data. If I forgot something, here is my chance to select the "back" button and then amend the information. All these screens simplify the IPAD evidence collection process and report writing process. The cancel button is good too because one might elect to do the process later if there was a problem where the examination process was being done. Suppose a fire alarm went off during the process, then later would be a good option. The help button is useful too because it provides additional documentation in the program. This is good because paper documentation can sometimes get separated from the examination machine.

Figure 6.8 – The Extracting Data Screen

This data extraction screen in figure 6.8 is very important because it provides a clear warning of what not to do, namely disconnecting cables. The green bar also informs the student or the examiner of the progress that has been made and how much more there is to do. This is important because seizing evidence is an important and stressful activity. An informative screen that simplifies the process and helps alleviate stress is good.

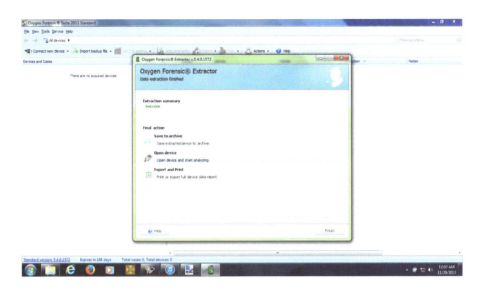

Figure 6.9 – The Data Extraction Finished With Success Screen

I like this screen because it shows success or any errors that might have occurred. We can see in figure 6.9 that there were not errors. There is also a help button, which is very important in case the student or investigator has a question about something in this step of the process. There is also a finish button that allows the person conducting the extraction of the IPAD evidence to progress to the end of the process. The advancing blue bar also provides information that helps keep the student or investigator informed.

Ms. L. says, "My niece is a lawyer and often talks about the deposition and expert witness process. The person who is a digital forensic examiner should be educated about the deposition process. In schools, computer forensic classes often focus on the technical issues concerning operating systems and file systems and do not focus on the bigger picture, which includes non-technical items such as the deposition process or presenting evidence in court. The deposition is a unique communication experience and the person who is going to give one should be educated about it ahead of time."

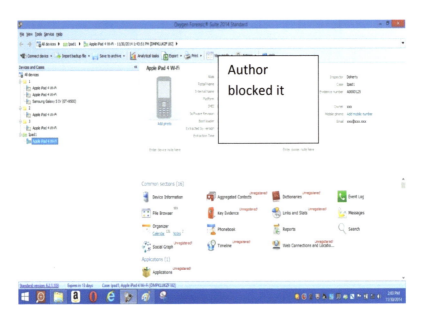

Figure 6.10 – The Results Page

This page has a variety of icons on the lower right side that help the student or investigator identify various aspects of device information and also get to key evidence quickly. The left side has a tree structure that also helps one navigate to evidence on more than one device if there is more than one device. The information about the device, any identifying numbers, and other important information are shown near the top of the screen. A panel that allows the student or investigator quick access to device information and evidence is very important and can help alleviate stress.

The other feature that the students and I find useful is the search. One can quickly look for keywords in the evidence that have to do with evidence. Search engines have become increasingly important as mobile devices have replaced traditional desktop computers and laptop computers for the younger generation. The IPAD, IPhone, and other mobile devices have large storage capacities, and that means more to look through.

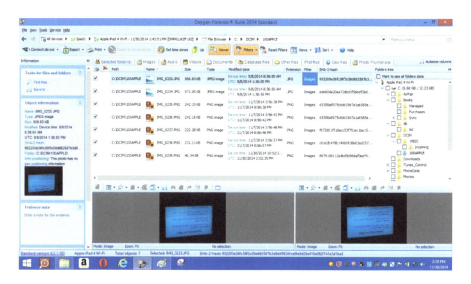

Figure 6.11 – Examples of Looking at Thumbnails of Evidence

Figure 6.11 shows the last of a long list of simulated evidence files. Another nice thing about many digital forensic tools is that they help to simplify the evidence previewing process. Each horizontal entry in figure 6.11 is a jpg or png file that contains a picture or graphic. When a horizontal entry is selected, the thumbnail appears near the bottom of the screen. The example of the depicted thumbnail in figure 6.11 shows an upside down PowerPoint slide from a malfunctioning data projector.

A student said that "Using the automated digital forensic tools is simpler than sifting through the plethora of simulated evidence on a large capacity storage device and creating a report." The student's remark is apropos because many people in the Discovery field have said that the legal industry has had to employ document readers because of the large volume of digital documents that need to be searched.

Final Remarks

When we teach a class on computer desktop forensics or IPAD forensics, there are so many technical, legal, procedural, and human factors that can emphasized. You have a lot of rich topics to choose from. Good luck!

Information About the Author's Previous Books

Eamon P. Doherty, PhD, CCE, SSCP, CPP, CISSP, is a Professor and the Cybercrime Training Lab director at Fairleigh Dickinson University (FDU), New Jersey. He also runs the Digital Forensics Special Interest Group (DFSIG) at the FDU Metropolitan Campus in Teaneck, New Jersey. He teaches continuing education, undergraduate, and graduate classes both on line and face to face. Dr. Doherty is a member of the High Tech Crimes Investigative Association (HTCIA) and ASIS International.

Dr. Eamon P. Doherty has written a number of books by himself or with coauthors on a wide range of topics. If you enjoy this book, you may wish to read some of his other works. Here is a brief synopsis of some of them.

Digital Forensics for Handheld Devices

This book was published by CRC Press in August of 2012. It has chapters that discuss digital forensics on a variety of handheld / mobile devices. It is numerous academic references and has been sold worldwide. The ISBN is 978-1439898772.

Tales of Cybercrime and Other Cyber Tales

This book was written by Eamon P. Doherty Ph.D. in an easy to understand edutainment format that teaches the reader about digital forensic, network security, and other cybercrime topics while entertaining the reader with fictional stories and characters. The book introduces the reader to a wide variety of topics in digital forensics, computer security, and investigation. The ISBN-13 is 978-1463402273. The book can be found for sale in a variety of online places such as eBay, Amazon, and Barnes and Noble. The publication date is May 2011. It is a quick read at 116 pages.

Emergency Management and Telemedicine for Everyone

This book was written by Eamon P. Doherty Ph.D., Gerard C. Muench Jr., and Gary Stephenson. This book is written in an easy to understand format and introduces the reader to a wide variety of topics in emergency management. It also discusses telemedicine as an aid to increase the quality of life for people living in remote areas that are far from a doctor and hospital. The ISBN-13 is 978-1425921293. The book can be found for sale in a variety of online places such as eBay, Amazon, and Barnes and Noble. The book is a large paperback edition and the publication date is April of 2006.

Computer Security and Telerobotics for Everyone

This book was written by Dr. Eamon P. Doherty and Joel Fernandes in 2005. The book was published by Authorhouse. The book discusses how Bruce Davis, a quadriplegic man, could operate a robotic arm with a Cyberlink Brain Body Interface and with a student made program. The book looks at the entire system as well as programming concepts. The ISBN is 978-1420896824.

Computer Recreation for Everyone

This book was written by Eamon P. Doherty Ph.D. and Gary Stephenson. The book presents a variety of computer games for people with and without disabilities. Some games are designed for pleasure or just passing time and having fun, while other games can be used to aid communication. The book also has numerous academic references where the reader can seek more information on a variety of topics introduced in each chapter. There are also chapters on games and virtual reality simulations that are used by mental health practitioners to help treat people with various phobias, such as fear of driving, fear of flying, and fear of heights. Another fascinating topic is how some navigation games such as "Snow World" are used with burn patients in order to pass time and to distract them from pain. This book is written in an easy to understand format and introduces the reader to a wide variety of topics in computer recreation, augmentative communication devices, and VR Mental Health. The ISBN-13 is 978-1420822397. The book is from 2005, 176 pages and in a 6x9 inch paperback format.

About The Author's Academic Papers

It is sometimes useful to see the author's published academic papers to get a further perspective on certain topics. Here is a partial list of published papers that have to do with digital forensics and emergency management.

E. P. Doherty and E. G. Doherty and E. Goei, "Using Forensic Images to Teach About White Collar Crime Online,"*2014 International Conference on e-Learning, e-Business, Enterprise Information Systems, and e-Government* (July 21-24, 2014, Las Vegas, USA). Conference Proceedings, Pages 22-25, ISBN 1-60132-268-2

E. P. Doherty, "Teaching IPAD Forensics Online with a MOOC,"*2014 International Conference on e-Learning, e-Business, Enterprise Information Systems, and e-Government* (July 21-24, 2014, Las Vegas, USA). Conference Proceedings, Pages 35-39, ISBN 1-60132-268-2

E. P. Doherty and E. G. Doherty and E. Goei, "Moving Legacy Device Forensics to an Online Format,"*2014 International Conference on e-Learning, e-Business, Enterprise Information Systems, and e-Government* (July 21-24, 2014, Las Vegas, USA). Conference Proceedings, Pages 57-63, ISBN 1-60132-268-2

E.P. Doherty, "New Challenges in Teaching e-Forensics Online," *WorldComp 2013 12th International Conference on e-Learning, e-Business, Enterprise Information Systems and e-Government*, July 22-25, 2013, Las Vegas, USA.

E. P. Doherty, "Teaching Mobile/GPS Forensics," *WorldComp 2012 Conference*, Las Vegas, Nevada, July 16-20, 2012., Conference Proceedings ISBN 1-60132-209-7, Pages 287-291

E. P. Doherty, "Teaching Cell Phone Forensics and E-Learning," *2011 International Conference on e-Learning, e-Business, Enterprise Information Systems, and e-Government* (EEE'11: July 18-21, 2011, Las Vegas, Nevada, USA). Conference Proceedings, Pages 161-165, ISBN 1-60132-176-7

E. P. Doherty, "Teaching Digital Camera Forensics in a Virtual Reality Classroom," *2011 International Conference on Computer Graphics and Virtual Reality* (CGVR'11: July 18-21, 2011, Las Vegas, Nevada, USA).

E. P. Doherty and E. G. Doherty, "E-Learning, Teaching Cell Phones Usage for Emergency Managers and First Responders,"*2011 International Conference on e-Learning, e-Business, Enterprise Information Systems, and e-Government* (July 18-21, 2011, Las Vegas, USA). Conference Proceedings, Pages 81-85, ISBN 1-60132-176-7

About the Author's Continuing Education Courses

The author has developed and taught a number of continuing education classes designed for both novices and those who have some experience with the topics. The following is a list of the courses along with a brief description of each class.

Introduction to Legacy Device Forensics - Continuing Education class developed and taught by Prof. Eamon P. Doherty, Ph.D., CCE, CPP, SSCP, CISSP. This three hour and fifteen minute class provides an opportunity for participants to learn about the vocabulary and tools used in the area of flip top cell phone forensics, IDE Hard Drive Forensics, Pager Systems Forensics (3.5 million people in the U.S. had pagers in 2012), CD and Floppy Drive Forensics and why such investigative knowledge is important for both businesses and security professionals. URL visited 1/1/2016 http://view2.fdu.edu/legacy/00000_CE_Dig_Forensics_Legacy.pdf

Introduction to IPAD Forensics - Continuing Education class developed and taught by Prof. Eamon P. Doherty, Ph.D., CCE, CPP, SSCP, CISSP. This three hour class is an opportunity to learn about the vocabulary and tools used in the field of IPAD Forensics (approx. 122 million people in the U.S. had an IPAD in 2013), and why such investigative knowledge is important for both businesses and security professionals. URL visited 1/1/2016 http://view2.fdu.edu/site-downloads/13098

Introduction to GPS Forensics - Continuing Education class developed and taught by Prof. Eamon P. Doherty, Ph.D., CCE, SSCP, CISSP. This introductory non-credit continuing education course consists of a brief survey of the various types of satellite navigation systems that exist in the world. The class also discusses some GPS navigation systems that can be used in an automobile and some of the tools that can be used to extract and map the data in these devices. URL http://view2.fdu.edu/legacy/00000_CE_Dig_Forensics_GPS.pdf

Cell Phone Seizure and Examination - Continuing Education class developed and taught by Prof. Eamon P. Doherty, Ph.D., CCE. This class is a half- day session that teaches a person about the tools and methods to seize digital forensic information from a phone and create a report. Reference URL visited 1/1/2016
http://view2.fdu.edu/legacy/ctlcellphoneforensicsflyer.pdf

Introduction to Digital Camera Forensics - Continuing Education class developed and taught by Prof. Eamon P. Doherty, Ph.D., CCE. This class is three hours in length that teaches a person about the tools and methods to seize / recover digital forensic information from a digital camera. Camera type and GPS location metadata in the pictures are also demonstrated. Reference URL visited 1/1/2016
http://view2.fdu.edu/legacy/00000_CE_Dig_Forensics_Camera.pdf

Introduction to Electronic Eavesdropping Device and Wiretap Detection - Continuing Education class developed and taught by Prof. Eamon P. Doherty, Ph.D., CCE. This class teaches the student about the various eavesdropping devices that exist and some of the TSCM equipment used to detect them. Some examples are demonstrated in class. Reference URL visited 1/1/2016
http://view2.fdu.edu/legacy/ctleavesdroppingforensicsflyer.pdf

www.ingramcontent.com/pod-product-compliance
Lightning Source LLC
Chambersburg PA
CBHW041153050326
40690CB00001B/453